AMAZING SCIENCE

AMAZING SOUND

Sally Hewitt

 Crabtree Publishing Company
www.crabtreebooks.com

Crabtree Publishing Company

www.crabtreebooks.com

Editors: L. Michelle Nielsen, Michael Hodge
Senior Editor: Joyce Bentley
Senior Design Manager: Rosamund Saunders
Designer: Tall Tree

Photo Credits: Karl-Heinz Haenel/zefa/Corbis: p. 21; Jon Hicks/Corbis: p. 7; Frans Lanting/Corbis: p. 19; Bruno Levy/zefa/Corbis: p. 17; NASA/Corbis: p. 6; David Pu'u/Corbis: p. 16; Robert Essel NYC/ Corbis: p. 23; Royalty-Free/Corbis: p. 20; Frank Blackburn/Ecoscene: p. 13; Joe McDonald/Getty Images: p. 22; Photographer's Choice/Getty Images: p. 10; Reportage/Getty Images: p. 12; Stone/Getty Images: cover, p. 8, p. 11, p. 14, p. 18, p. 24, p. 25, p. 27; The Image Bank/Getty Images: p. 26, David Tipling/Getty Images: p. 15; Mel Yates/Getty Images: p. 3, p. 9

Activity & illustrations: Shakespeare Squared pp. 28-29.

Cover: A grizzly bear is on its hind legs, growling.

Title page: A boy plays a beat on his drums.

Library and Archives Canada Cataloguing in Publication

Hewitt, Sally, 1949-
    Amazing sound / Sally Hewitt.

(Amazing science)
Includes index.
ISBN 978-0-7787-3615-8 (bound)
ISBN 978-0-7787-3629-5 (pbk.)

    1. Sound--Juvenile literature. I. Title. I. Series: Hewitt, Sally, 1949- . Amazing science.

QC225.5.H49 2007   j534   C2007-904310-0

Library of Congress Cataloging-in-Publication Data

Hewitt, Sally, 1949-
  Amazing sound / Sally Hewitt.
    p. cm. -- (Amazing science)
  Includes index.
  ISBN-13: 978-0-7787-3615-8 (rlb)
  ISBN-10: 0-7787-3615-6 (rlb)
  ISBN-13: 978-0-7787-3629-5 (pb)
  ISBN-10: 0-7787-3629-6 (pb)
  1. Sound--Juvenile literature. I. Title. II. Series.

QC225.5.H43 2008
534--dc22
                                        2007027462

Crabtree Publishing Company

www.crabtreebooks.com   1-800-387-7650

Printed in the U.S.A./102016/CG20160822

Published in Canada
Crabtree Publishing
616 Welland Ave.
St. Catharines, ON
L2M 5V6

Published in the United States
Crabtree Publishing
PMB 59051
350 Fifth Avenue, 59th Floor
New York, New York 10118

Published by CRABTREE PUBLISHING COMPANY
Copyright © **2008**

Contents

Amazing sound   6

Vibrations   8

Ears   10

Loud and quiet   12

Low and high   14

Big and small   16

Traveling sound   18

Near and far   20

Echoes   22

Music   24

Sending sound   26

Sound in action   28

Glossary   30

Index   32

Amazing sound

The moon is **quiet** and still. There is no **air** to make **sounds** and no wind to blow the dust on the moon's surface.

Sound is made by **moving** air, so without air, there is no sound.

Earth is surrounded by air. It is a noisy, busy place.

YOUR TURN!

Listen. What can you hear? Do you know what is making the sounds you hear?

Traffic, rain hitting umbrellas, and people talking are all familiar sounds.

SCIENCE WORDS: air   quiet   sound

Vibrations

A humming bird beats its wings so fast that they look like a blur. The wings move the air, and we **hear** it as a hum.

People hear sounds when moving air goes into their **ears**.

When a drum is hit, the air around it **vibrates**, or moves very fast. The moving air makes the sound.

YOUR TURN!

Put your hand on the television while it is on. Can you feel the vibrations?

When a drummer plays a beat, vibrating air goes into our ears as a sound.

SCIENCE WORDS: **hear**   **vibrations**

9

Ears

A herd of elephants walks through the savanna. Their enormous ears **listen** for danger.

Ears are **shaped** so they can pick up sounds.

People and animals hear with their ears. Our ears help us hear sounds all around us.

YOUR TURN!

Cup your hand around your ear to make it bigger. Can you hear better now?

We use our ears to hear our friends talk.

SCIENCE WORDS: ears shaped

Loud and quiet

Loud sounds can damage your ears. Workers at airports and air-force bases wear equipment that protects their ears from the sounds of jets.

The ear drum and tiny bones inside your ears vibrate when sound goes into your ears.

Quiet sounds are made by small vibrations in the air, and loud sounds are made by large vibrations.

YOUR TURN!

Clap loudly. Clap quietly. What do you do to make a loud and quiet clap?

Mice make quiet sounds.

SCIENCE WORDS: **loud   quiet**

13

Low and high

A bear's **low** growl rumbles through the forest. It scatters deer and can scare birds out of the trees.

People and animals make sounds with the **voice boxes** in their throats.

High sounds are made by fast vibrations. Low sounds are made by slow vibrations.

YOUR TURN!

Gently feel the voice box in your throat while you make low and high sounds. What happens to it?

A small bird makes a high sound when it sings.

SCIENCE WORDS: **high   low   voice box**

Big and small

Enormous waves roll onto a beach. They break onto the sand with loud crashing sounds.

When waves are big, loud sounds are made.

When waves are small, they make quiet sounds. You have to listen carefully to hear them.

YOUR TURN!

*Why do you think a **still** pool of water makes no sound at all?*

When the sea is calm and quiet, it only moves a little.

SCIENCE WORDS: move   still

Traveling sound

In a thunderstorm, flashes of lightning split the sky. A few seconds later, thunder crashes with a loud bang.

Light **travels** faster than sound does so lightning is seen before the bang of thunder is heard.

Sound needs something to travel **through**. It travels through air, water, the ground, and even walls.

YOUR TURN!

Listen. What have the sounds that you hear traveled through to reach your ears?

The sound of whales singing to each other travels through water.

SCIENCE WORDS: listen   through   travel

Near and far

A truck rumbles along the highway. Its engine sounds louder as it gets **closer**.

The closer you are to a noise, the louder it sounds.

Sound seems quieter as it travels through the air. A noise coming from **far** away sounds quiet.

As an airplane goes up in the sky, it seems quieter.

SCIENCE WORDS: **far   near**

21

Echoes

Bats dart through the night sky catching insects to eat. They use their ears to find insects in the dark.

The sound of a bat's squeak hits an insect and **bounces** back into the bat's ears as an **echo**.

The bat then knows where the insect is to catch it.

When you shout in a cave, your voice bounces off the walls, and you hear an echo.

YOUR TURN!

Bounce a ball off a wall to see how an echo works. Your voice bounces back off the wall just like a ball.

SCIENCE WORDS: **bounce** **echo**

Music

Musicians blow, bang, pluck, and shake **instruments** to make sounds. These sounds make music.

Air in tubes, strings, and drum skins vibrates when instruments are played.

Short strings play high **notes**, and longer strings play lower notes.

YOUR TURN!

Make instruments. Put rice, beans, or pasta into containers with lids. Shake them, and hear the different sounds.

Cello players press the strings with their fingers to make the strings shorter.

SCIENCE WORDS: **instruments   notes**

Sending sound

Your voice can travel to **satellites** in space and back to Earth, which lets you talk to someone far away.

The sound of your voice is sent from a telephone to satellites on invisible **radio waves**.

You can also make telephone calls through **wires** called "land lines".

Your voice can travel from telephone to telephone along wires.

YOUR TURN!

Do you think that a cellular phone sends sounds along wires or radio waves?

Sound in action

Try this experiment so you can easily see how we hear sounds!

What you need

- large rubber band
- large tin can
- wooden ruler
- pencil
- plastic wrap
- small tin can
- paper
- tablespoon of ground coffee

1. Pull the plastic wrap tightly over the open end of the large tin can. Use the rubber band to secure the plastic wrap over the top of the can.

2. Sprinkle coffee onto the plastic wrap that is stretched over the can. Make sure that the coffee is spread evenly in a very thin layer over all of the plastic wrap.

3. Hold the small tin can about an inch above the coffee. Make sure that the open end of the small can is pointing toward the coffee. Tap the side of the small tin can with the wooden ruler. Do this several times. Try moving the small can farther away from the plastic wrap, or tapping it harder. What changes?

4. What is happening to the coffee? Why do you think this happens? Record your observations on a piece of paper.

What happened:

Sound travels in waves. When we hear sound, those waves are hitting our ear drums. This is how we hear birds singing and thunder cracking. As you tap the side of the small can with the ruler, you are producing sound waves. These waves travel in all directions. When these waves make contact with the plastic wrap, it causes the coffee to vibrate. The large can is functioning just like an ear, and the plastic wrap is just like an ear drum. By making the coffee move, you have just seen sound in action!

Glossary

air   An invisible gas that is all around us.

bounce   To hit something and jump back off of it quickly.

close   Something is close when it is nearby. Close is the opposite of far.

ears   The parts of your body that you hear with.

echo   You hear an echo when the sound of your voice bounces off of something and goes back into your ears.

far   When something is far, it is a long way away.

hear   You hear when sounds go into your ears.

high   A sound that is the opposite of deep. A bird singing is a high sound.

instruments   Something that you blow, bang, pluck, or shake to make musical sounds.

listen   To pay attention to sounds.

loud   A sound that is strong and easy to hear. A road drill and thunder make loud sounds.

low   A sound that is deep. A bear growling and a big drum make low sounds.

move   Something is moving when it is not still.

notes   Notes are musical sounds made by singing or by a musical instrument.

quiet   A little noise or no noise at all.

radio waves   Invisible waves in the air that carry sound.

satellite   An object that goes around Earth in space, receiving messages from Earth and sending messages back.

shaped   Everything has a shape. Ears are shaped so that they can pick up sounds easily.

sound   A noise that is made when the air vibrates.

still   When things are not moving, they are still.

through   When you go through something, you pass through the middle of it.

travel   To go from one place to another.

vibrates   Making tiny, very fast movements.

voice box   The part of your body that makes sounds when you speak.

wire   A long string made of metal.

Index

air 6, 7, 8, 9, 13, 19, 21,
  25, 28, 29

bang 18, 19, 24, 28
blow 6, 24, 28

close 20, 28

drum 9, 25, 29

ear drum 13
ears 9, 10, 11, 12, 13, 19,
  22, 23, 28, 28
echo 24, 25, 30
engine 22

growl 14, 29

hear 7, 8, 9, 11, 19, 21, 23,
  25, 28
high 14, 15, 25, 28

instruments 24, 25, 28, 29

loud 12, 13, 16, 17, 18, 20,
  21, 28
low 14, 15, 25, 29

music 24, 28

noise 7, 21, 29
notes 25, 29

quiet 6, 7, 12, 13, 17,
  21, 29

radio waves 27, 29

shake 24, 25, 28
shout 23
sing 15, 19, 28, 29
slow 15

talk 7, 11, 21, 26
throat 15
thunder 18, 19
thunderstorm 18

vibrate 9, 13, 25, 29
vibration 8, 13, 15
voice 21, 23, 26, 27
voice box 15, 29

waves 16, 17
wind 6